TRAINING COST ANALYSIS

A how-to guide for trainers and managers

By Glenn E. Head

Social Architect, New World Design Center
Box 4488, Boulder, Colorado 80306

Revised and updated

ASTD

AMERICAN SOCIETY
FOR TRAINING AND
DEVELOPMENT

1640 KING STREET
BOX 1443
ALEXANDRIA, VIRGINIA
22313-2043

703/683-8100
FAX 703/683-8103

Ordering information: Books published by the American Society for Training and Development can be ordered by calling 703/683-8100.

Library of Congress Catalog Card Number: 93-74581

ISBN: 1-56286-000-3

Illustrated by Gail Joy Hoag

ASTD

AMERICAN SOCIETY FOR TRAINING AND DEVELOPMENT

1640 KING STREET
BOX 1443
ALEXANDRIA, VIRGINIA
22313-2043

703/683-8100
FAX 703/683-8103

Preface

In 1986, the National Society for Performance and Instruction honored *Training Cost Analysis* as the Outstanding Instructional Communication of the year, a highly competitive award. The award "recognizes an outstanding instructional communication which enables individuals and/or organizations to apply systematic approaches to achieve excellence in human performance."

In addition to its use by training practitioners and managers in hundreds of organizations around the world, numerous institutions of higher learning have adopted *Training Cost Analysis* as a learning tool for their students.

Professional journals have praised the author's work with such words as: "Glenn Head has written a book that allows a user with no prior costing experience to produce an analysis that is unlikely to overlook any major cost consideration" (*Journal of Computer Based Instruction*, Winter 1986, Vol. 13, No. 1, p. 25).

ASTD is pleased to offer this revised and updated edition of a book that is a genuine, practical guide for trainers, training managers, and others who need to identify and compare training costs in their organizations.

Contents

Foreword

Chaos, unexpected change, and anticipated change are realities in every organization today. Through the Total Quality movement almost everybody has become familiar with benchmarking as a system of determining progress in our ever changing world. In the training profession we apply systems aimed at supporting workers in doing their jobs more efficiently and effectively within the unknown parameters of chaos. My first conversations and thinking on concepts like just-in-time delivery, performance support systems, and imbedded systems training began in the mid 1970s in my work as a behavioral scientist with the Air Force Human Resources Laboratory's Technical Training Division. And it was there I learned first hand of the incredible resistance to change we have in organizations and ourselves.

I learned that even if an organization wanted to change its approach to training, no benchmarks existed from which one could measure progress. My job in the Air Force was to invent (or discover) these benchmarks where none had previously existed. The single, most widely recognized benchmark became cost. And when I discovered that few could identify the cost of existing training in either their government or civilian organizations I decided to write this book.

I don't want you to think that just because one has a clear picture of the cost of existing training, and proposes an alternative that is significantly more efficient, that the alternative will be or should be chosen. The *effectiveness* of the approach must guide all training design decisions. Although this seems obvious, I have discovered that many organizations simply don't choose to increase their performance effectiveness. Today I notice how difficult change is on the personal level and until each of us as an individual is willing to change our beliefs, to become a learning individual or a learning organism/organization, there will be no significant change.

This book is the result of over 18 years of experience in the analysis of training cost— and of the contributions from many individuals. Especially deserving of acknowledgement are Charles C. (Chuck) Buchanan and Lori Gillespie. Their support of my work personally and assistance in the formulation of these concepts is ongoing and treasured. Also Marian Saunders, then Manager of Educational Development at the U.S. Senate Computer Center in Washington, D.C., applied this guide in a major pre-publication test and provided support that made this book possible. Today Marian is my partner in life.

We work as Social Architects, dedicated to helping people and their organizations achieve their full potential. Each year we help several organizations who choose to go beyond business as usual to begin their process of discovering the full potential of their people and their organization.

Glenn E. Head
P.O. Box 4488
Boulder, Colorado 80306
303/443-6868

1. Overview

**What can using the
Training Cost Model do for me?**

**How does the
Training Cost Model work?**

**What's the best way
for me to use this guide?**

NOTES

What can using the Training Cost Model do for me?

Using the Training Cost Model, which is the core of this guide to training cost analysis, you will be able to:
■ identify the costs of existing training programs,
■ project the costs of proposed training programs, and
■ compare the costs of using different methods for the same training.

This guide is a simple—but comprehensive—tool that guides you through the process necessary for effective, cost-conscious decision making.

This guide will help you conduct the research to justify a training expenditure or a program change—and then to communicate this justification graphically and authoritatively to supervisors and other corporate decision makers.

How does the Training Cost Model work?

The Model is a series of mathematical formulas into which you enter data. It permits you to calculate the actual cost of training on a per course and per student basis. Printed worksheets will guide you step-by-step through your analysis.

1 + 1 = **PRODUCT EFFICIENCY**

What's the best way for me to use this guide?

First, as you skim through the text and examine the worksheets, you will see an example to walk you through your first cost analysis. A column is provided on the worksheets where you may make notes about your own situation—or you may choose to write directly on the extra worksheets provided in the Appendix. The data gathering will be fairly extensive; you will recognize early the importance of careful documentation and organization of your information sources. Accuracy will be rewarded, although changes can readily be made later, if necessary.

After skimming through the text and examining the worksheets, you'll be ready to follow the example through the Training Cost Model.

READY!

2. The Example

A hypothetical—but typical—
example of a company in need of
training cost analysis.

This example is expanded and used
throughout the book to illustrate
the use of the cost model.

NOTES

In this section we begin to examine a hypothetical but typical example of how using this practical guide can simplify your training decision-making. XYZ Company is contemplating conversion of an existing instructor-led, group-paced training course to a self-paced, computer-based course. You are the corporate training manager and you must make a recommendation to the budget committee. Here is the background:

 **VS**

The Example

XYZ is a large manufacturer of computers and storage peripherals. Your customers range from national accounts including *Fortune* 500 companies to small, high-technology companies. XYZ maintains customer service and support offices in ten major U.S. cities.

The existing training course is designed for XYZ's entry-level technicians. It has been taught for the past year at the XYZ World Headquarters Training Center in Boulder, Colorado; it is expected to last approximately three more years. The course is eight days long and is taught once a month. Twenty students attend each class. Each student is allotted two days for round-trip travel to Boulder.

Your company has been extremely successful this past year, resulting in growth problems. Some customers have been waiting for delivery of XYZ's new computer and call the company daily to inquire about the date their orders will be filled. There is such a backlog of orders that the manufacturing plant is working three shifts.

The load on the installation and maintenance technicians is heavy. Whenever a technician leaves the work center to attend training sessions, the remaining workers suffer from overload. To meet the demands placed on them, they work overtime, for which they receive double-time pay. Without overtime, deliveries and installations fall behind schedule and cost the company more in lost sales and bad customer relations.

This situation has cost XYZ dearly. Citing sloppy maintenance and servicing on existing XYZ equipment, four major customers have cancelled their orders for $5 million each in new business—a loss to date of $20 million in sales for XYZ.

One of your staff members has recommended that the existing installation and maintenance training course be converted to an individualized, computer-based training course to save time, wear and tear on personnel, and money. The cost of a computer system to support this one course, including the necessary instructional design and course development, is estimated at $550,000. The course time would be reduced to approximately four days and computer-based simulation would replace most of the equipment currently required in the training room. Additionally, the system could support other courses—but this in turn would place new demands upon your training and management staff.

What would you recommend? How would you make your decision?

Obviously, Training Cost Analysis would be your guide to determine the cost effectiveness of your proposed program. In order to do this, you must *first* determine the cost of your *existing* program.

LET'S BEGIN

NOTES

3. Basic Cost Factors

Student Costs
+
Instructor Costs
+
Instructional Development Costs
+
Facilities Costs
+
Maintenance Costs

NOTES

A thorough training cost analysis takes into consideration each of these five areas:

$$ student costs
$$ instructor costs
$$ instructional development costs
$$ facilities costs
$$ maintenance costs

In order to arrive at the costs in each of these areas, it is necessary to identify basic cost factors. The following is a list that includes some primary considerations. It is by no means exhaustive, and in fact we will discuss additional cost factors as we proceed with the analysis.

Basic Cost Factors

- Expected course life
- Course length
- Number of students in each class
- Number of times the course is held
- Geographic location of the course
- Average annual salaries
- Company's fringe benefits percentage
- Annual productive days
- Average travel and per diem expenses
- Number of instructors per class
- Lost opportunity costs
- Production and materials costs
- Development and evaluation time

With the background information we have so far on the XYZ Company, we can already fill in some of the blanks on the Basic Cost Factors Worksheet. Feel free to jot down any data you already have about one of your training programs in the extra column provided, or use the Basic Cost Factors Worksheet located in the Appendix.

It will require some research to fill in the remaining blanks. Next we'll gather more data on the XYZ Company and provide you with guidance in gathering your own data.

Basic Cost Factors

	XYZ	Your Program
• Course medium:	lecture/lab	
• Expected course life:	4 years	
• Course length:	8 days + 2 travel	
• Number in each class:	20	
• Times course held each year:	12	
• Geographic location of course:	Boulder, CO	
• Facilities costs:		
• Average annual salary:		
Students		
Instructors		
Instructional designers		
Subject matter experts		
Clerical staff		
Project leader		
Manager		
• Annual productive days:		
• Company's fringe benefits %:		
• Average per diem expenses:		
Students		
Instructors		
• Average travel expenses:		
Students		
Instructors		
• Number of instructors per class:		
• Development time:		
Project leader		
Instructional designer		
Subject matter expert		
Manager		
Clerical		
• Administrative time:		
Manager		
Clerical		
• Production costs:		
• Materials costs:		
One-time		
Consumable		
• Evaluation costs:		
• Revision %:		

17

NOTES

4. Data Gathering

Documenting Data Sources

Data Worksheets

XYZ Data Gathering

NOTES

It's important to have a system to keep track of your sources and methods of calculation. Which system you choose is not important, as long as you use one! Below is an example of a format you may find helpful in keeping track of your data. Jotting down each piece of information on a separate large index card gives you plenty of flexibility. If you prefer, you may use the data worksheets provided in the Appendix.

Date_____

Course_____

Cost factor _____

Contact_____

Phone _____

Final data to be entered on worksheet_____

The Training Cost Model is organized into the five major cost areas: Student Costs, Instructor Costs, Instructional Development Costs, Facilities Costs, and Maintenance Costs. Let's collect the data for XYZ Company in each of these areas.

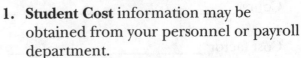

1. **Student Cost** information may be obtained from your personnel or payroll department.

XYZ's student technicians earn an average of $30,000 annually. The corporate overhead rate of 30% covers fringe benefits excluding vacation and holiday pay. Each student gets 10 paid vacation days per year, plus 12 paid holidays and 5 sick days.

Each trainee is paid $75 per day to cover meals and lodging. The average round-trip airfare and local transportation to Boulder is $450 (taking into consideration all the locations from which the technicians travel). The average round-trip travel time is two days.

Basic Cost Factors

	XYZ	Your Program
• Course medium:	lecture/lab	
• Expected course life:	4 years	
• Course length:	8 days + 2 travel	
• Number in each class:	20	
• Times course held each year:	12	
• Geographic location of course:	Boulder, CO	
• Facilities costs:		
• Average annual salary:		
Students	$30,000	
Instructors		
Instructional designers		
Subject matter experts		
Clerical staff		
Project leader		
Manager		
• Annual productive days:	234	
• Company's fringe benefits %:	30%	
• Average per diem expenses:		
Students	$75	
Instructors		
• Average travel expenses:		
Students	$450	
Instructors		
• Number of instructors per class:		
• Development time:		
Project leader		
Instructional designer		
Subject matter expert		
Manager		
Clerical		
• Administrative time:		
Manager		
Clerical		
• Production costs:		
• Materials costs:		
One-time		
Consumable		
• Evaluation costs:		
• Revision %:		

2. **Instructor Cost** data may be found in your personnel or payroll department, as well.

   XYZ's instructors earn $35,000 annually.

   All instructors live in Boulder; they receive no per diem or travel reimbursements. Because of the hands-on nature of this course, two instructors are required to teach and provide assistance to students in each class.

3. **Instructional Development Costs** may be obtained from the training department.

   The development team that designed the training program consisted of a project leader, two instructional designers, and a subject matter expert (SME). The project leader's salary is $40,000 per year. The project leader spent 90 staff days on the project. The average of the instructional designers' salaries is $37,000 per year. The instructional designers spent 150 staff days each (300 staff days total) from needs analysis through beta test on the project. The SME's salary is $35,000 per year; he spent 20 staff days on the project.

   As corporate training manager, you spent approximately 15 percent of your time managing this development project over a period of eight months. Your annual salary is $46,000.

Basic Cost Factors

	XYZ	Your Program
• Course medium:	lecture/lab	
• Expected course life:	4 years	
• Course length:	8 days + 2 travel	
• Number in each class:	20	
• Times course held each year:	12	
• Geographic location of course:	Boulder, CO	
• Facilities costs:		
• Average annual salary:		
Students	$30,000	
Instructors	**$35,000**	
Instructional designers	**$37,000**	
Subject matter experts	**$35,000**	
Clerical staff		
Project leader	**$40,000**	
Manager	**$46,000**	
• Annual productive days:	234	
• Company's fringe benefits %:	30%	
• Average per diem expenses:		
Students	$75	
Instructors	**$0**	
• Average travel expenses:		
Students	$450	
Instructors	**$0**	
• Number of instructors per class:	**2**	
• Development time:		
Project leader	**90 staff days**	
Instructional designer	**300 staff days**	
Subject matter expert	**20 staff days**	
Manager	**15% x 8 months**	
Clerical		
• Administrative time:		
Manager		
Clerical		
• Production costs:		
• Materials costs:		
One-time		
Consumable		
• Evaluation costs:		
• Revision %:		

The clerical group spent 50 percent of its time over eight months on this project. Two people are in this group; one earns $19,000 and the other earns $15,000 annually.

The production costs, including all videotape costs, totalled $10,515. The two computer systems required for hands-on exercises total $156,000. Another $10,328 was needed for computer materials.

The course evaluation costs totalled $3,000. This included $1,200 in travel costs and $1,800 in instructional designer and student salaries.

4. **Facilities Costs** may be available from your operations department.

The annual cost per square foot for the World Headquarters building is $17. The 1,000-square-foot training room is a combination of traditional seats with desks and a laboratory housing the computer equipment. The space is used solely for this training course. The cost to design, build and furnish the training room was $15,000. The training room is expected to last five more years before it needs any further renovation.

Basic Cost Factors

	XYZ	Your Program
• Course medium:	lecture/lab	
• Expected course life:	4 years	
• Course length:	8 days + 2 travel	
• Number in each class:	20	
• Times course held each year:	12	
• Geographic location of course:	Boulder, CO	
• Facilities costs:	**$20,000**	
• Average annual salary:		
Students	$30,000	
Instructors	$35,000	
Instructional designers	$37,000	
Subject matter experts	$35,000	
Clerical staff	**$17,000**	
Project leader	$40,000	
Manager	$46,000	
• Annual productive days:	234	
• Company's fringe benefits %:	30%	
• Average per diem expenses:		
Students	$75	
Instructors	$0	
• Average travel expenses:		
Students	$450	
Instructors	$0	
• Number of instructors per class:	2	
• Development time:		
Project leader	90 staff days	
Instructional designer	300 staff days	
Subject matter expert	20 staff days	
Manager	15% x 8 months	
Clerical	**50% x 8 months**	
• Administrative time:		
Manager		
Clerical		
• Production costs:	**$10,515**	
• Materials costs:		
One-time	**$166,328**	
Consumable		
• Evaluation costs:	**$3,000**	
• Revision %:		

5. Maintenance Costs, including administrative costs, consumable materials and revision costs, may be derived from the experience of your training department.

a. **Administrative Costs.**
As manager of corporate training for XYZ Company, you estimate that approximately 2% of your time is spent attending to this course. Your salary is $46,000. In addition, you estimate that approximately 10% of the clerical group's time is required to support this course. There are two clerks; one earns $15,000 and the other earns $19,000.

b. **Consumable Materials.**
The company provides student materials for each student, including a workbook and several job aids. The cost of these materials is $6 per student.

c. **Revision/Update Costs.**
The development team estimated that the course would require approximately 10 percent in revisions per year unless major modifications were made to the computer hardware being manufactured. No funds were budgeted for major modifications.

Basic Cost Factors

	XYZ	Your Program
• Course medium:	lecture/lab	
• Expected course life:	4 years	
• Course length:	8 days + 2 travel	
• Number in each class:	20	
• Times course held each year:	12	
• Geographic location of course:	Boulder, CO	
• Facilities costs:	$20,000	
• Average annual salary:		
Students	$30,000	
Instructors	$35,000	
Instructional designers	$37,000	
Subject matter experts	$35,000	
Clerical staff	$17,000	
Project leader	$40,000	
Manager	$46,000	
• Annual productive days:	234	
• Company's fringe benefits %:	30%	
• Average per diem expenses:		
Students	$75	
Instructors	$0	
• Average travel expenses:		
Students	$450	
Instructors	$0	
• Number of instructors per class:	2	
• Development time:		
Project leader	90 staff days	
Instructional designer	300 staff days	
Subject matter expert	20 staff days	
Manager	15% x 8 months	
Clerical	50% x 8 months	
• Administrative time:		
Manager	**2%**	
Clerical	**10%**	
• Production costs:	$10,515	
• Materials costs:		
One-time	$166,328	
Consumable	**$6/Student**	
• Evaluation costs:	$3,000	
• Revision %:	**10%**	

Still more data will be required as we proceed through the Model's formulas. Within each of the following sections on the five major cost areas, plenty of guidance will be provided.

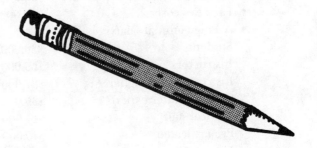

Basic Cost Factors

	XYZ	Your Program
• Course medium:	lecture/lab	
• Expected course life:	4 years	
• Course length:	8 days + 2 travel	
• Number in each class:	20	
• Times course held each year:	12	
• Geographic location of course:	Boulder, CO	
• Facilities costs:	$20,000	
• Average annual salary:		
Students	$30,000	
Instructors	$35,000	
Instructional designers	$37,000	
Subject matter experts	$35,000	
Clerical staff	$17,000	
Project leader	$40,000	
Manager	$46,000	
• Annual productive days:	234	
• Company's fringe benefits %:	30%	
• Average per diem expenses:		
Students	$75	
Instructors	$0	
• Average travel expenses:		
Students	$450	
Instructors	$0	
• Number of instructors per class:	2	
• Development time:		
Project leader	90 staff days	
Instructional designer	300 staff days	
Subject matter expert	20 staff days	
Manager	15% x 8 months	
Clerical	50% x 8 months	
• Administrative time:		
Manager	2%	
Clerical	10%	
• Production costs:	$10,515	
• Materials costs:		
One-time	$166,328	
Consumable	$6/Student	
• Evaluation costs:	$3,000	
• Revision %:	10%	

BASIC COST FACTORS

NOTES

5. Student Costs

Salaries
+
Fringe Benefits
+
Productive Days
+
Per Diem
+
Travel
+
Lost Opportunity

NOTES

80%

Student costs are often overlooked when calculating the cost of training. However, experience has shown that student costs often represent more than 80 percent of the cost of a training program. Performance Support Systems incorporating just-in-time training or embedded training concepts may have a significant impact on course length, especially if they are well conceived and teach only what is necessary for the specific task. Changing training variables such as course length can affect student costs dramatically, and thus significantly affect your overall cost of training.

The following procedure will guide you through your use of the Cost Model—either to follow the XYZ Company's analysis or to conduct your own. (All XYZ Company calculations are rounded to the nearest dollar.) All totals are for a one-year period.

The lower case letters that identify the paragraphs in the text correspond with the letters on the Worksheets. You may use the extra columns on the Worksheets in the text for your own notes or use the blank Worksheets in the Appendix.

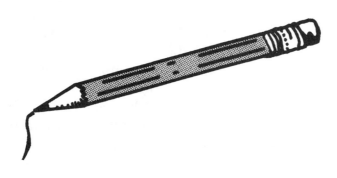

Procedure

a. Enter the **Student Annual Salary** on Line **a** of the Worksheet.

    In the XYZ example, the average student annual salary is $30,000. (You will have your own information on Basic Cost Factors or Data Worksheets.)

b. Multiply the Student Annual Salary by your company's **Fringe Benefits Factor**. This total represents what it costs your company to have its employees available to work for one year.

    Fringe benefits generally amount to between 25% and 75% of an employee's salary. We add the fringe benefits percentage, say 25%, to total salary, 100%, to arrive at the Fringe Benefits Factor of 125% or 1.25.

    In the XYZ example, the fringe benefits percentage is 30%, for a fringe benefits factor of 130% or 1.30.

c. Divide by the number of **Annual Productive Days** per year.

    To calculate the annual productive days, first add the number of vacation days and holidays the student is allocated each year. Then subtract that number from 261 (365 days minus 104 days for 52 weekends). For example, suppose the student is entitled to 12 paid holidays, 10 vacation days, and 5 days sick leave. Subtract these 27 days from 261 to arrive at the number of productive working days per year—234.

Student Costs Worksheet

XYZ Company _____

a.	Student Annual Salary		_30,000_	(a) _____
b.	Fringe Benefits Factor	x	_1.30_	(b) _____
c.	Annual Productive Days	÷	_____	(c) _____
d.	Student Daily Salary	=	_____	(d) _____
e.	Student Per Diem	+	_____	(e) _____
f.	Class Length (days)	x	_____	(f) _____
g.	Salary Per Student Per Class	=	_____	(g) _____
h.	Student Travel Costs	+	_____	(h) _____
i.	Lost Opportunity Cost	+	_____	(i) _____
j.	Total Number of Students	x	_____	(j) _____
k.	Student Costs Subtotal	=	_____	(k) _____
l.	Miscellaneous Student Costs	+	_____	(l) _____
m.	**Total Student Costs (Annual)**	=	_____	**(m)** _____

In the XYZ example, students are able to work 234 days per year.

d. The result of these calculations is the **Average Student Daily Salary**.

e. Add the **Student Per Diem**, or reimbursable daily expenses for housing, meals and tips, to the daily salary. You may usually obtain an average of these costs from your payroll or accounting office.

In the XYZ example, students receive an average of $75 per day for lodging, meals and tips.

f. Multiply by the **Class Length** in days, *including travel time.* In determining class length, consider the number of days in the course plus an estimate of the amount of time students spend traveling to and from the training course location. This may include both air and automobile travel. If your students are traveling varying amounts of time, average the total time. If students travel only a few hours *but do not attend work on those days*, count travel time as an entire day. It is important to include the total amount of time the student is absent from the job. If the course is self-instructional, use the average student completion time.

In the XYZ example, we estimated that the class length is 8 days and round trip travel time is 2 days for a total of 10 days.

Student Costs Worksheet

XYZ Company _____

a.	Student Annual Salary		_30,000_	(a) _____
b.	Fringe Benefits Factor	x	_1.30_	(b) _____
c.	Annual Productive Days	÷	_234_	(c) _____
d.	Student Daily Salary	=	_122_	(d) _____
e.	Student Per Diem	+	_75_	(e) _____
f.	Class Length (days)	x	_10_	(f) _____
g.	Salary Per Student Per Class	=	_____	(g) _____
h.	Student Travel Costs	+	_____	(h) _____
i.	Lost Opportunity Cost	+	_____	(i) _____
j.	Total Number of Students	x	_____	(j) _____
k.	Student Costs Subtotal	=	_____	(k) _____
l.	Miscellaneous Student Costs	+	_____	(l) _____
m.	**Total Student Costs (Annual)**	=	_____	(m) _____

g. When this calculation is completed, we have determined the student salary and per diem on a per student basis for a 10-day class.

h. Add the **Student Travel Costs** including round-trip air, bus or train fare, local automobile mileage, taxi or local public transportation costs. You may average these costs, but document the method you use to calculate this figure.

   In the XYZ example, students spend an average of $450 for a round-trip airfare ticket and ground transportation to the training course location.

i. Enter the **Lost Opportunity Cost** per student per day. This is the value of the reduced productivity or time lost due to the student's absence from the job. Although difficult to obtain, this figure is significant and necessary. There are several ways to calculate it.

   In some cases, when students attend training classes, temporary personnel are hired to substitute on the job. In this case, calculate the lost opportunity cost (LO) as the daily salary cost of the temporary replacement personnel salary (TS) multiplied by the number of students (NS) and the class length (CL).

$$LO = TS \times NS \times CL$$

Student Costs Worksheet

XYZ Company   _____

a.	Student Annual Salary		_30,000_	(a) _____
b.	Fringe Benefits Factor	x	_1.30_	(b) _____
c.	Annual Productive Days	÷	_234_	(c) _____
d.	Student Daily Salary	=	_167_	(d) _____
e.	Student Per Diem	+	_75_	(e) _____
f.	Class Length (days)	x	_10_	(f) _____
g.	Salary Per Student Per Class	=	_2,420_	(g) _____
h.	Student Travel Costs	+	_450_	(h) _____
i.	Lost Opportunity Cost	+	_____	(i) _____
j.	Total Number of Students	x	_____	(j) _____
k.	Student Costs Subtotal	=	_____	(k) _____
l.	Miscellaneous Student Costs	+	_____	(l) _____
m.	**Total Student Costs (Annual)**	=	_____	(m) _____

Temporary personnel who do not perform as well as the students they replace may cause a slowdown on the job. This occurs more often on production lines and in service call positions. If this is the case, you may want to estimate a slowdown factor of anywhere from 1.2 to 1.5 (with 1.5 equivalent to sleepwalking). Then multiply the temporary personnel salary (TS) by the number of students (NS) by the class length (CL) by the slowdown factor (SF).

$$LO = TS \times NS \times CL \times SF$$

Or, you may calculate the lost opportunity cost by determining the amount of dollars each employee contributes to the gross revenue of the organization. This is especially appropriate for sales personnel. By dividing the gross revenue earned per employee (GR) by the number of Annual Productive Days (APD), and then multiplying this figure by the number of days in the training course (CL), you can determine the value of productivity lost (LO) while the employee is a student in your course.

$$LO = (GR \div APD) \times CL$$

You may encounter a situation where other company employees are simply overworked to "cover" while another employee is in training. This makes calculation of lost opportunity cost especially challenging. We encourage you to be creative in finding a quantitative value representing

Student Costs Worksheet

XYZ Company _____

a. Student Annual Salary	_30,000_	(a) _____
b. Fringe Benefits Factor	x _1.30_	(b) _____
c. Annual Productive Days	÷ _234_	(c) _____
d. Student Daily Salary	= _167_	(d) _____
e. Student Per Diem	+ _75_	(e) _____
f. Class Length (days)	x _10_	(f) _____
g. Salary Per Student Per Class	= _2,420_	(g) _____
h. Student Travel Costs	+ _450_	(h) _____
i. Lost Opportunity Cost	+ _____	(i) _____
j. Total Number of Students	x _____	(j) _____
k. Student Costs Subtotal	= _____	(k) _____
l. Miscellaneous Student Costs	+ _____	(l) _____
m. Total Student Costs (Annual)	= _____	(m) _____

the amount of overwork. Perhaps quality declines, or reject rates increase, or customer complaints increase.

In the XYZ example, we determined that double-time pay is required to compensate for staff hours lost in training. We double the Student Daily Salary ($167) and multiply it by the class length (10) to find the lost opportunity cost of $3,340.

j. Multiply by the **Total Number of Students** who annually take the training course. If this course is to replace an existing one, just use the same number of students as attend regularly now. If this is a proposed training course, estimate the number of students based on the employee target population, similar courses given, or perhaps marketing or planning data.

In the XYZ example, we estimated that 20 students attend each class and that 12 classes a year are offered. The total number of students per year is therefore 240.

k. When the multiplication is completed, this represents the annual **Student Cost Subtotal** for this training course.

l. Calculate any **Miscellaneous Student Costs**.

The weekend expenses of this XYZ course are calculated by multiplying the per diem rate of $75 by two days (Saturday and Sunday), multiplied again by the annual number of students (240) or $36,000.

Student Costs Worksheet

XYZ Company _____

a.	Student Annual Salary		_30,000_	(a) _____
b.	Fringe Benefits Factor	x	_1.30_	(b) _____
c.	Annual Productive Days	÷	_234_	(c) _____
d.	Student Daily Salary	=	_167_	(d) _____
e.	Student Per Diem	+	_75_	(e) _____
f.	Class Length (days)	x	_10_	(f) _____
g.	Salary Per Student Per Class	=	_2,420_	(g) _____
h.	Student Travel Costs	+	_450_	(h) _____
i.	Lost Opportunity Cost	+	_3,340_	(i) _____
j.	Total Number of Students	x	_240_	(j) _____
k.	Student Costs Subtotal	=	_1,490,400_	(k) _____
l.	Miscellaneous Student Costs	+	_36,000_	(l) _____
m.	**Total Student Costs (Annual)**	=	_1,526,400_	(m) _____

STUDENT COSTS WORKSHEET

m. Add Line **k** and Line **l**; this represents
Total Student Costs (annual).

6. Instructor Costs

Salaries

+

Fringe Benefits

+

Productive Days

+

Per Diem

+

Travel

+

Lost Opportunity

NOTES

Instructor costs are an obvious expense of any instructor-led or monitored training program. The data needed and the actual calculations are very similar to those for student costs.

The lower case letters that identify the paragraphs in the following text correspond to the letters on the Worksheets in this section and in the Appendix. (All XYZ Company calculations are rounded to the nearest dollar.)

Procedure

a. Enter the **Instructor Annual Salary** on Line **a**.

   In the XYZ example, the instructor's annual salary is $35,000.

b. Multiply the instructor salary by the **Fringe Benefits Factor**.

   In the XYZ example, the fringe benefits factor is 1.30.

c. Divide by the number of **Annual Productive Days**.

   In the XYZ example, annual productive days total 234.

d. The result is the **Instructor Daily Salary**.

e. Add to this the **Instructor Per Diem Cost**, or the reimbursable daily housing, meals and tips expense. This figure is usually available from the payroll or accounting office.

In the XYZ example, we determined that the instructors all work at the training course location, so they have no reimbursable expenses.

f. Now multiply by the **Class Length** (in days, including travel time.) Travel time may be an average.

In the XYZ example, the class length (which includes no travel time for the instructors) is 8 days.

g. The result is the **Salary Per Instructor Per Class**.

h. Multiply by the **Number of Classes** per year.

In the XYZ example, the number of classes per year is 12.

i. Add the **Instructor Travel Costs**, including round-trip air, bus, or train fare, taxi, auto mileage, or local public transportation costs. The costs may be averaged.

If the instructor travels more than once during the year, multiply the number of trips by the travel cost per trip to arrive at an annual cost.

In the XYZ example, all instructors live in the same city as the training site location; they had no reimbursable expenses.

j. Add the **Lost Opportunity Cost** per instructor per day. This is the value of the productive time lost because an instructor is absent from another aspect of his or her job.

Instructor Costs Worksheet

			XYZ Company		
a.	Instructor Annual Salary		_35,000_	(a)	
b.	Fringe Benefits Factor	x	_1.30_	(b)	
c.	Annual Productive Days	÷	_234_	(c)	
d.	Instructor Daily Salary	=	_194_	(d)	
e.	Instructor Per Diem	+	_0_	(e)	
f.	Class Length (days)	x	_8_	(f)	
g.	Salary Per Instructor Per Class	=	_1,552_	(g)	
h.	Number of Classes	x	_12_	(h)	
i.	Instructor Travel Costs	+	_0_	(i)	
j.	Lost Opportunity Cost	+		(j)	
k.	Total Number of Instructors	x		(k)	
l.	Instructor Costs Subtotal	=		(l)	
m.	Miscellaneous Instructor Costs	+		(m)	
n.	**Total Instructor Costs (Annual)**	=		**(n)**	

The techniques illustrated to calculate the lost opportunity cost for students may be applied to instructors. The question of what instructors would be doing if their time in the classroom were increased or decreased must be addressed in terms of its impact upon corporate productivity or revenue.

In the XYZ example, the instructors are experienced maintenance technicians and their skills are in high demand within the company. For each day an instructor is back in the field, the need for overtime pay for other workers is reduced by an amount equal to at least one-half his or her daily salary. (This is equivalent to two hours a day of overtime at double-time pay.) Therefore, the lost opportunity cost is equal to one-half the instructor's daily average salary ($194 x 50%) multiplied by the number of days the instructor is not in the field (class length, 8 x number of classes, 12 or 96 days).

Lost opportunity cost for instructors is one of the most difficult areas for which to assign a value. You are encouraged not to overlook it simply because it may be difficult or time consuming. Be creative in your approach and stay in your comfort zone with your assumptions.

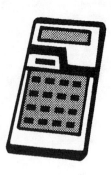

k. Multiply by the **Total Number of Instructors**, including part-time and "on-call" instructors, required to teach the course.

Instructor Costs Worksheet

			XYZ Company		
a.	Instructor Annual Salary		_35,000_	(a)	
b.	Fringe Benefits Factor	x	_1.30_	(b)	
c.	Annual Productive Days	÷	_234_	(c)	
d.	Instructor Daily Salary	=	_194_	(d)	
e.	Instructor Per Diem	+	_0_	(e)	
f.	Class Length (days)	x	_8_	(f)	
g.	Salary Per Instructor Per Class	=	_1,552_	(g)	
h.	Number of Classes	x	_12_	(h)	
i.	Instructor Travel Costs	+	_0_	(i)	
j.	Lost Opportunity Cost	+	_9,312_	(j)	
k.	Total Number of Instructors	x	_2_	(k)	
l.	Instructor Costs Subtotal	=		(l)	
m.	Miscellaneous Instructor Costs	+		(m)	
n.	**Total Instructor Costs (Annual)**	=		**(n)**	

In the XYZ example, two full-time instructors are required per class.

l. The result represents the **Instructor Cost Subtotal** for the year.

m. Add the **Miscellaneous Instructor Costs**. In the XYZ example, there are none.

n. The result is the **Total Instructor Costs** (annual).

This completes the Instructor Costs section. Review your own entries to see if they match your Basic Cost Factors and Data Worksheets.

Instructor Costs Worksheet

			XYZ Company		
a.	Instructor Annual Salary		35,000	(a)	
b.	Fringe Benefits Factor	x	1.30	(b)	
c.	Annual Productive Days	÷	234	(c)	
d.	Instructor Daily Salary	=	194	(d)	
e.	Instructor Per Diem	+	0	(e)	
f.	Class Length (days)	x	8	(f)	
g.	Salary Per Instructor Per Class	=	1,552	(g)	
h.	Number of Classes	x	12	(h)	
i.	Instructor Travel Costs	+	0	(i)	
j.	Lost Opportunity Cost	+	9,312	(j)	
k.	Total Number of Instructors	x	2	(k)	
l.	Instructor Costs Subtotal	=	55,872	(l)	
m.	Miscellaneous Instructor Costs	+	0	(m)	
n.	**Total Instructor Costs (Annual)**	=	55,872	(n)	

INSTRUCTOR COSTS WORKSHEET

NOTES

7. Instructional Development Costs

Personnel
+
Production
+
Materials
+
Evaluation

NOTES

Although most cost categories deal with ongoing costs, instructional development costs are generally one-time expenses that must be amortized over the expected life of the course. Entire books have been written on the instructional development process. This book is designed simply to provide you with guidelines to determine what data should be collected—and to show you how to calculate your training costs.

First we calculate the personnel costs involved in the instructional development process. Then we will add the production, materials, and evaluation costs.

In determining salary expenses in this section you may find it useful to break down the daily rate into an hourly rate and use hours instead of days. Simply divide the daily rate by the number of productive working hours per day in your organization. The accounting or industrial engineering division may be able to provide you with the appropriate number of hours to use for your organization. (This number is usually 6 or less, but the critical element is for all interested parties to agree as to the number of hours.)

The lower case letters that identify the paragraphs in the following text correspond to the letters on the Worksheets in this section and in the Appendix. (All XYZ calculations are rounded to the nearest dollar.)

a
b c e
d

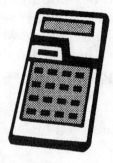

Procedure

a. Enter the **Project Leader Annual Salary**.
    In the XYZ example, the project leader's salary is $40,000 per year.

b. Multiply by the **Fringe Benefits Factor**.
    In the XYZ example, the fringe benefits factor is 1.30.

c. Divide by the number of **Annual Productive Days**.
    This is 234 in the XYZ example.

d. The result is the **Project Leader Daily Salary**.

e. Now multiply the project leader daily salary by the amount of time that the project leader spent or is expected to spend on the project. You may have to estimate the amount of time the project leader has spent on an existing program or will spend on a new project. If the project leader has other responsibilities, only consider time spent acting as project leader.
    In the XYZ example, the project leader spent 90 days on the project.

f. The result is the **Project Leader Costs**.

Instructional Development
Personnel Costs Worksheet

XYZ Company

a.	Project Leader Annual Salary	_40,000_	(a)
b.	Fringe Benefits Factor	x _1.30_	(b)
c.	Annual Productive Days	÷ _234_	(c)
d.	Project Leader Daily Salary	= _222_	(d)
e.	Number of Days on Project	x _90_	(e)
f.	**Project Leader Costs**	= _20,000_	**(f)**
g.	Inst. Designer Annual Salary		(g)
h.	Fringe Benefits Factor	x	(h)
i.	Annual Productive Days	÷	(i)
j.	Inst. Designer Daily Salary	=	(j)
k.	Number of Days on Project	x	(k)
l.	**Instructional Designer Costs**	=	**(l)**
m.	Subj. Matter Exp. Annual Salary		(m)
n.	Fringe Benefits Factor	x	(n)
o.	Annual Productive Days	÷	(o)
p.	SME Daily Salary	=	(p)
q.	Number of Days on Project	x	(q)
r.	**Subject Matter Expert Costs**	=	**(r)**
s.	Manager Annual Salary		(s)
t.	Fringe Benefits Factor	x	(t)
u.	Annual Productive Days	÷	(u)
v.	Manager Daily Salary	=	(v)
w.	Number of Days on Project	x	(w)
x.	**Manager Costs**	=	**(x)**
y.	Clerical Annual Salary		(y)
z.	Fringe Benefits Factor	x	(z)
aa.	Annual Productive Days	÷	(aa)
bb.	Clerical Daily Salary	=	(bb)
cc.	Number of Days on Project	x	(cc)
dd.	**Clerical Costs**	=	**(dd)**
ee.	**Total Instructional Development Personnel Costs**	=	**(ee)**

g. Enter the **Instructional Designer Annual Salary**. If there is more than one designer and they are paid at different rates, average their salaries.

In the XYZ example, the instructional designers' average salary is $37,000 per year.

h. Multiply by the **Fringe Benefits Factor**.

In the XYZ example, the fringe benefits factor is 1.30.

i. Divide by the number of **Annual Productive Days**.

This is 234 in the XYZ example.

j. The result is the **Instructional Designer Daily Salary**.

k. Multiply by the number of staff days spent or estimated to be spent on the project.

You may need to estimate the total amount of time that the instructional designers will spend developing the training course. You may have some guidelines based on previous development efforts. Don't forget time for needs analysis. If the project leader is also an instructional designer, determine the percentage of time spent only on developing the training course.

Remember to count staff working days and not calendar days. You may require 80 staff days in 2 months, which amounts to 2 full-time designers for 2 months.

Instructional Development
Personnel Costs Worksheet

XYZ Company   _____

a.   Project Leader Annual Salary   _____   (a) _____
b.   Fringe Benefits Factor   x _____   (b) _____
c.   Annual Productive Days   ÷ _____   (c) _____
d.   Project Leader Daily Salary   = _____   (d) _____
e.   Number of Days on Project   x _____   (e) _____
f.   Project Leader Costs   = *20,000*   **(f)** _____

g.   Inst. Designer Annual Salary   *37,000*   (g) _____
h.   Fringe Benefits Factor   x *1.30*   (h) _____
i.   Annual Productive Days   ÷ *234*   (i) _____
j.   Inst. Designer Daily Salary   = *206*   (j) _____
k.   Number of Days on Project   x _____   (k) _____
l.   Instructional Designer Costs = _____   **(l)** _____

m.   Subj. Matter Exp. Annual Salary   _____   (m) _____
n.   Fringe Benefits Factor   x _____   (n) _____
o.   Annual Productive Days   ÷ _____   (o) _____
p.   SME Daily Salary   = _____   (p) _____
q.   Number of Days on Project   x _____   (q) _____
r.   Subject Matter Expert Costs = _____   **(r)** _____

s.   Manager Annual Salary   _____   (s) _____
t.   Fringe Benefits Factor   x _____   (t) _____
u.   Annual Productive Days   ÷ _____   (u) _____
v.   Manager Daily Salary   = _____   (v) _____
w.   Number of Days on Project   x _____   (w) _____
x.   Manager Costs   = _____   **(x)** _____

y.   Clerical Annual Salary   _____   (y) _____
z.   Fringe Benefits Factor   x _____   (z) _____
aa.   Annual Productive Days   ÷ _____   (aa) _____
bb.   Clerical Daily Salary   = _____   (bb) _____
cc.   Number of Days on Project   x _____   (cc) _____
dd.   Clerical Costs   = _____   **(dd)** _____
ee.   Total Instructional Develop-
     ment Personnel Costs   = _____   **(ee)** _____

%

A number of rules of thumb have been used in the industry. Our experience is offered as a guide only. For each of the types of training listed below, there is a corresponding ratio. The ratio represents the number of development hours estimated for each resulting hour of student learning time.

Instructional Method	Estimated Ratio
Traditional instructor-led class	20-1
Self-instructional print	80-1
Interactive computer assisted instruction (without programming* or simulation)	300-1
Computer simulation with high level of graphics	500-1

*(Programming costs vary widely for various computer hardware configurations and also depend to a great extent upon the availability of supporting authoring languages or systems.)

In the XYZ example, Instructional Designers spent 300 staff days on the project.

1. The result is total **Instructional Designer Costs**.

Instructional Development
Personnel Costs Worksheet

XYZ Company _____

a.	Project Leader Annual Salary		_____	(a) _____
b.	Fringe Benefits Factor	x	_____	(b) _____
c.	Annual Productive Days	÷	_____	(c) _____
d.	Project Leader Daily Salary	=	_____	(d) _____
e.	Number of Days on Project	x	_____	(e) _____
f.	**Project Leader Costs**	=	*20,000*	**(f)** _____

g.	Inst. Designer Annual Salary		*37,000*	(g) _____
h.	Fringe Benefits Factor	x	*1.30*	(h) _____
i.	Annual Productive Days	÷	*234*	(i) _____
j.	Inst. Designer Daily Salary	=	*206*	(j) _____
k.	Number of Days on Project	x	*300*	(k) _____
l.	**Instructional Designer Costs**	=	*61,800*	**(l)** _____

m.	Subj. Matter Exp. Annual Salary		_____	(m) _____
n.	Fringe Benefits Factor	x	_____	(n) _____
o.	Annual Productive Days	÷	_____	(o) _____
p.	SME Daily Salary	=	_____	(p) _____
q.	Number of Days on Project	x	_____	(q) _____
r.	**Subject Matter Expert Costs**	=	_____	**(r)** _____

s.	Manager Annual Salary		_____	(s) _____
t.	Fringe Benefits Factor	x	_____	(t) _____
u.	Annual Productive Days	÷	_____	(u) _____
v.	Manager Daily Salary	=	_____	(v) _____
w.	Number of Days on Project	x	_____	(w) _____
x.	**Manager Costs**	=	_____	**(x)** _____

y.	Clerical Annual Salary		_____	(y) _____
z.	Fringe Benefits Factor	x	_____	(z) _____
aa.	Annual Productive Days	÷	_____	(aa) _____
bb.	Clerical Daily Salary	=	_____	(bb) _____
cc.	Number of Days on Project	x	_____	(cc) _____
dd.	**Clerical Costs**	=	_____	**(dd)** _____
ee.	**Total Instructional Development Personnel Costs**	=	_____	**(ee)** _____

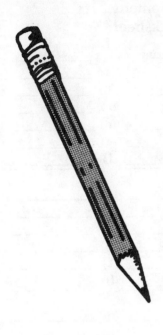

m. Enter the **Subject Matter Expert Annual Salary**. If there is more than one subject matter expert and they are paid at different rates, average their salaries.

   In the XYZ example, the subject matter expert's salary is $35,000 per year.

n. Multiply by the **Fringe Benefits Factor**.
   In the XYZ example, the fringe benefits factor is 1.30.

o. Divide by the number of **Annual Productive Days**.
   This is 234 in the XYZ example.

p. The result is the **Subject Matter Expert (SME) Daily Salary**.

q. Multiply by the number of staff days spent or estimated to be spent on the project. You may have to estimate the amount of time the subject matter expert has spent on an existing program or will spend on a new project.

   In the XYZ example, subject matter experts spent approximately 20 days on the project.

r. The result is **Subject Matter Expert Costs**.

Instructional Development Personnel Costs Worksheet

XYZ Company _____

a.	Project Leader Annual Salary		_____	(a) _____
b.	Fringe Benefits Factor	x	_____	(b) _____
c.	Annual Productive Days	÷	_____	(c) _____
d.	Project Leader Daily Salary	=	_____	(d) _____
e.	Number of Days on Project	x	_____	(e) _____
f.	**Project Leader Costs**	=	_20,000_	**(f)** _____
g.	Inst. Designer Annual Salary		_____	(g) _____
h.	Fringe Benefits Factor	x	_____	(h) _____
i.	Annual Productive Days	÷	_____	(i) _____
j.	Inst. Designer Daily Salary	=	_____	(j) _____
k.	Number of Days on Project	x	_____	(k) _____
l.	**Instructional Designer Costs**	=	_61,800_	**(l)** _____
m.	Subj. Matter Exp. Annual Salary		_35,000_	(m) _____
n.	Fringe Benefits Factor	x	_1.30_	(n) _____
o.	Annual Productive Days	÷	_234_	(o) _____
p.	SME Daily Salary	=	_194_	(p) _____
q.	Number of Days on Project	x	_20_	(q) _____
r.	**Subject Matter Expert Costs**	=	_3,889_	**(r)** _____
s.	Manager Annual Salary		_____	(s) _____
t.	Fringe Benefits Factor	x	_____	(t) _____
u.	Annual Productive Days	÷	_____	(u) _____
v.	Manager Daily Salary	=	_____	(v) _____
w.	Number of Days on Project	x	_____	(w) _____
x.	**Manager Costs**	=	_____	**(x)** _____
y.	Clerical Annual Salary		_____	(y) _____
z.	Fringe Benefits Factor	x	_____	(z) _____
aa.	Annual Productive Days	÷	_____	(aa) _____
bb.	Clerical Daily Salary	=	_____	(bb) _____
cc.	Number of Days on Project	x	_____	(cc) _____
dd.	**Clerical Costs**	=	_____	**(dd)** _____
ee.	**Total Instructional Development Personnel Costs**	=	_____	**(ee)** _____

s. Enter the **Manager Annual Salary**.
    In the XYZ example, the manager's salary is $46,000 per year.

t. Multiply by the **Fringe Benefits Factor**. (This factor may be different for managers; check with your personnel or accounting department.)
    In the XYZ example, the fringe benefits factor is 1.30.

u. Divide by the number of **Annual Productive Days**.
    This is 234 in the XYZ example.

v. The result is the **Manager Daily Salary**.

w. Now multiply the Manager Daily Salary by the number of days that the manager spent or is expected to spend on the project. You may have to estimate the amount of time the manager has spent on an existing program or will spend on a new project.
    In the XYZ example, the manager spent 15 percent of his or her time over eight months or 23.4 days. Divide Annual Productive Days (234) by 12 months, then multiply by the number of months over which the project extended (8). Then multiply by 15% to calculate the number of manager days on the project.

x. The result is the **Manager Costs**.

Instructional Development Personnel Costs Worksheet

XYZ Company _____

a.	Project Leader Annual Salary		_____	(a) _____
b.	Fringe Benefits Factor	x	_____	(b) _____
c.	Annual Productive Days	÷	_____	(c) _____
d.	Project Leader Daily Salary	=	_____	(d) _____
e.	Number of Days on Project	x	_____	(e) _____
f.	**Project Leader Costs**	=	*20,000*	**(f)** _____
g.	Inst. Designer Annual Salary		_____	(g) _____
h.	Fringe Benefits Factor	x	_____	(h) _____
i.	Annual Productive Days	÷	_____	(i) _____
j.	Inst. Designer Daily Salary	=	_____	(j) _____
k.	Number of Days on Project	x	_____	(k) _____
l.	**Instructional Designer Costs**	=	*61,800*	**(l)** _____
m.	Subj. Matter Exp. Annual Salary		_____	(m) _____
n.	Fringe Benefits Factor	x	_____	(n) _____
o.	Annual Productive Days	÷	_____	(o) _____
p.	SME Daily Salary	=	_____	(p) _____
q.	Number of Days on Project	x	_____	(q) _____
r.	**Subject Matter Expert Costs**	=	*3,889*	**(r)** _____
s.	Manager Annual Salary		*46,000*	(s) _____
t.	Fringe Benefits Factor	x	*1.30*	(t) _____
u.	Annual Productive Days	÷	*234*	(u) _____
v.	Manager Daily Salary	=	*256*	(v) _____
w.	Number of Days on Project	x	*23.4*	(w) _____
x.	**Manager Costs**	=	*5,990*	**(x)** _____
y.	Clerical Annual Salary		_____	(y) _____
z.	Fringe Benefits Factor	x	_____	(z) _____
aa.	Annual Productive Days	÷	_____	(aa) _____
bb.	Clerical Daily Salary	=	_____	(bb) _____
cc.	Number of Days on Project	x	_____	(cc) _____
dd.	**Clerical Costs**	=	_____	**(dd)** _____
ee.	**Total Instructional Development Personnel Costs**	=	_____	**(ee)** _____

y. Enter the **Clerical Annual Salary**.
In the XYZ example, the clerks' salaries are $15,000 and $19,000. The average is $17,000.

z. Multiply by the **Fringe Benefits Factor**.
(This factor may be different for clerical personnel; check with your personnel or accounting department.)
In the XYZ example, the fringe benefits factor is 1.30.

aa. Divide by the number of **Annual Productive Days**.
This is 234 in the XYZ example.

bb. The result is the **Clerical Daily Salary**.

cc. Now multiply the Clerical Daily Salary by the amount of time that the clerks spent or are expected to spend on the project. You may have to estimate the amount of time the clerks have spent on an existing program or will spend on a new program.
In the XYZ example, the clerks spent 50 percent of their time over 8 months, or 156 staff days on the project. (Divide 234 by 12, then multiply by 8, then multiply by 50%, then multiply by 2 clerks.)

dd. The result is the **Clerical Costs**.

ee. Add the Project Leader Costs (Line **f**), Instructional Designer Costs (Line **l**), Subject Matter Expert Costs (Line **r**), Manager Costs (Line **x**), and Clerical Costs (Line **dd**). The result is the total **Instructional Development Personnel Cost**.

Instructional Development Personnel Costs Worksheet

XYZ Company _____

a.	Project Leader Annual Salary		_____	(a) _____
b.	Fringe Benefits Factor	x	_____	(b) _____
c.	Annual Productive Days	÷	_____	(c) _____
d.	Project Leader Daily Salary	=	_____	(d) _____
e.	Number of Days on Project	x	_____	(e) _____
f.	**Project Leader Costs**	=	*20,000*	**(f)** _____
g.	Inst. Designer Annual Salary		_____	(g) _____
h.	Fringe Benefits Factor	x	_____	(h) _____
i.	Annual Productive Days	÷	_____	(i) _____
j.	Inst. Designer Daily Salary	=	_____	(j) _____
k.	Number of Days on Project	x	_____	(k) _____
l.	**Instructional Designer Costs**	=	*61,800*	**(l)** _____
m.	Subj. Matter Exp. Annual Salary		_____	(m) _____
n.	Fringe Benefits Factor	x	_____	(n) _____
o.	Annual Productive Days	÷	_____	(o) _____
p.	SME Daily Salary	=	_____	(p) _____
q.	Number of Days on Project	x	_____	(q) _____
r.	**Subject Matter Expert Costs**	=	*3,889*	**(r)** _____
s.	Manager Annual Salary		_____	(s) _____
t.	Fringe Benefits Factor	x	_____	(t) _____
u.	Annual Productive Days	÷	_____	(u) _____
v.	Manager Daily Salary	=	_____	(v) _____
w.	Number of Days on Project	x	_____	(w) _____
x.	**Manager Costs**	=	*5,990*	**(x)** _____
y.	Clerical Annual Salary		*17,000*	(y) _____
z.	Fringe Benefits Factor	x	*1,30*	(z) _____
aa.	Annual Productive Days	÷	*234*	(aa) _____
bb.	Clerical Daily Salary	=	*94*	(bb) _____
cc.	Number of Days on Project	x	*156*	(cc) _____
dd.	**Clerical Costs**	=	*14,664*	**(dd)** _____
ee.	**Total Instructional Development Personnel Costs**	=	*106,343*	**(ee)** _____

a. Now transfer the Instructional Development Personnel Costs (Line **ee**) onto Line **a** of the Instructional Development Costs Worksheet.

b. Add the **Production and Materials Costs** related to designing the training course. This may include the cost of talent for audio or videotapes, art work, equipment rental, programming costs, software costs for computer-assisted instruction, word processing, etc.

    All books, videotapes, computer disks, audio tapes, reproduction fees, and other materials costs belong in this category. Included here is the cost of any required classroom equipment such as computers, slide projectors, video recorders, simulators, etc. *Not included* are consumable handouts or training manuals distributed to students in the course.

    In the XYZ example, we add $10,515 in production costs, $156,000 for computer equipment, and $10,328 for computer materials. The total is $176,843.

c. Add the **Evaluation Costs** for the training course.

    Usually one formative review, test and revision cycle is included as part of the estimated development hours used in determining personnel costs. However, depending upon how well the first test succeeds and how rigorous the testing, additional testing or evaluation may be warranted.

Instructional Development Costs Worksheet

XYZ Company _____

a. Personnel Costs   _106,343_   (a) _____

b. Production and Materials Costs   + _176,843_   (b) _____

c. Evaluation Costs   + _____ (c) _____

d. Instructional Development
Subtotal   = _____ (d) _____

e. Misc. Instructional Development
Costs   + _____ (e) _____

f. Instructional Development Costs   = _____ (f) _____

g. Amortization   ÷ _____ (g) _____

h. **Total Instructional Development
Costs Per Year**   = _____ **(h)** _____

Since delivery and implementation of the final training course should be done only after a pilot test has been completed, be sure to account for the pilot test cost in this part of your analysis. Also include costs for all testing beyond the first formative evaluation. This may include costs related to small-group testing, prototype materials, and travel and per diem costs required to test the materials. Beware of underestimating the significance or the cost of this critical step in the development process.

In the XYZ example, there were two formal evaluation points—a large group test and a pilot test of the training course. Since the testing was performed at a remote location, travel costs of $1,200 were incurred. Instructional designer, project leader, clerical and student salaries during the testing period amounted to $1,800. The sum of these two components is $3,000.

d. To arrive at the **Instructional Development Subtotal**, add together the major cost factors. These include Personnel Costs, Production and Materials Costs, and Evaluation Costs.

e. Add the **Miscellaneous Instructional Development Costs** that do not fit elsewhere in the Model.

There are no miscellaneous instructional development costs in the XYZ example.

Instructional Development Costs Worksheet

XYZ Company

a. Personnel Costs   _106,343_ (a) _____

b. Production and Materials Costs   + _176,843_ (b) _____

c. Evaluation Costs   + _3,000_ (c) _____

d. Instructional Development Subtotal   = _286,186_ (d) _____

e. Misc. Instructional Development Costs   + _0_ (e) _____

f. Instructional Development Costs   = _____ (f) _____

g. Amortization   ÷ _____ (g) _____

h. **Total Instructional Development Costs Per Year**   = _____ **(h)** _____

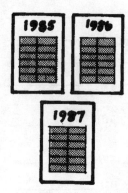

f. The result is the **Instructional Development Costs**.

g. **Amortization**. Divide by the number of years you expect the course to be taught.

Instructional Development Costs are a one-time expense. It is appropriate to amortize these costs over the expected life of the course. If you are unfamiliar with this process, ask your accounting department for guidance.

In the XYZ example, the course is expected to be taught for four years.

h. The result is the **Total Instructional Development Costs Per Year**.

That concludes the Instructional Development Costs section. Review your own entries.

Instructional Development Costs Worksheet

	XYZ Company		
a. Personnel Costs	_106,343_	(a)	
b. Production and Materials Costs	+ _176,843_	(b)	
c. Evaluation Costs	+ _3,000_	(c)	
d. Instructional Development Subtotal	= _286,186_	(d)	
e. Misc. Instructional Development Costs	+ _0_	(e)	
f. Instructional Development Costs	= _572,412_	(f)	
g. Amortization	÷ _4_	(g)	
h. Total Instructional Development Costs Per Year	= _143,103_	**(h)**	

NOTES

8. Facilities Costs

NOTES

The information needed to determine facilities costs may be difficult to obtain. But the overall contribution to total training cost of facilities is usually very small, so we do not recommend that you spend a great deal of time gathering this data—unless you have made or are intending to make a major investment in your training facility.

The lower case letters that identify the paragraphs in the following text correspond with the letters on the Worksheets. (All XYZ Company calculations are rounded to the nearest dollar.)

Procedure

a. Calculate the **Annual Facilities Costs**. This includes mortgage or rent, utilities, maintenance, security, and any other building administration factors. If space is leased, many of these factors will be included in the cost per square foot. This information may be obtained from your accounting or operations department.

Also included is the cost of any furnishing or remodeling of the training classroom.

In the XYZ example, space costs $17 per square foot multiplied by 1,000 square feet for a total of $17,000 per year. It cost $15,000 to furnish and remodel the training classroom, which is expected to last five years. Dividing the cost of remodeling and furnishing the classroom by the expected life will amortize this cost. In the example, dividing $15,000 by 5 years results in a $3,000 annual amortized expense to add to the annual square-foot cost of $17,000 for a total of $20,000.

b. Multiply the Annual Facilities Costs by the percentage of time the room is allocated for your course.

In the XYZ example, the specialized training equipment needed makes this room unusable for any other purpose. Therefore, the entire facility cost is allocated to this course.

c. The result is the **Total Facilities Costs**.

That completes the Facilities Costs. Review your entries.

Facilities Costs Worksheet

XYZ Company   _____

a. Annual Facilities Costs   _____ *20,000* _____ (a) _____

b. Course Allocation   x _____ *100%* _____ (b) _____

c. Total Facilities Costs   = _____ *20,000* _____ (c) _____

NOTES

9. Maintenance Costs

Administrative

+

Consumable Materials

+

Revision Factor

NOTES

Maintenance costs begin after the course is fully developed and implemented. They can be categorized by three cost areas:
- administrative,
- consumable materials, and
- revisions.

Administrative Costs take into consideration the amount of time spent on your course each year by managers and clerical staff. (This is separate and apart from the time managers and clerical staff spend during the instructional development project.)

Procedure

a. Enter the **Manager Annual Salary**. (If there is more than one manager, perform calculations **a** through **d** for each one and total them.)

   In the XYZ example, the manager's annual salary is $46,000.

b. Multiply Manager Annual Salary by the **Fringe Benefits Factor**.

   In the XYZ example, the fringe benefits factor is 1.30.

c. Now multiply by the **Percent of Manager's Time** allocated to the course.

   In the XYZ example, approximately 2 percent of the manager's time is related to the administration of this course. Therefore we multiply by 0.02.

d. The result is the **Manager Costs Per Year**. (Remember to include data for all managers who are involved with this program.)

87

%

e. Next, the clerical costs are calculated. These are the clerical and secretarial costs directly related to training administration. Examples of such activities are typing student records and filing. Depending on the company, this will usually take between 5% and 12% of the clerical staff's time. The first item is the **Clerical Annual Salary**.

In the XYZ example, there are two clerks. Although one is primarily responsible for supporting this course, the other backs him or her up. The average of their salaries is $17,000.

f. Multiply the Clerical Annual Salary by the **Fringe Benefits Factor**.

In the XYZ example, the factor is 1.30.

g. Now multiply by the **Percent of Clerical Time** allocated to the course.

In the XYZ example, the clerical staff spends 10% of its time supporting this course, so we multiply by 0.1.

h. The result is the **Clerical Costs Per Year**.

i. Add the **Manager Costs Per Year** (same as Line **d**).

j. The result is the **Total Administrative Costs Per Year**.

Take a few minutes to review your entries.

Administrative Costs Worksheet

		XYZ Company	
a. Manager Annual Salary		46,000	(a)
b. Fringe Benefits Factor	x	1.30	(b)
c. Percent of Manager's Time	x	.02	(c)
d. Manager Costs Per Year	=	1,196	(d)
e. Clerical Annual Salary		17,000	(e)
f. Fringe Benefits Factor	x	1.30	(f)
g. Percent of Clerical Time	x	0.1	(g)
h. Clerical Costs Per Year	=	2,210	(h)
i. Manager Costs Per Year	+	910	(i)
j. Total Administrative Costs	=	3,406	(j)

Consumable Materials Costs include workbooks, note pads and other materials that students either use up during the course or take home with them afterward. It also includes materials and services used in the preparation of these student materials. For a computer-based training network, it may include telecommunications charges.

Procedure

a. Enter the **Number of Students** in each class.

> In the XYZ example there are 20 students per class.

b. Multiply by the **Consumable Materials Costs** for each student.

> In the XYZ example, consumable materials cost $6 per student. They include copies of the documentation and procedures manuals.

c. Multiply by the **Number of Classes** held each year.

> In the XYZ example, 12 classes are held each year.

d. The result is the **Consumable Materials Subtotal**.

e. Add any miscellaneous materials costs that you can identify. Paper, pencils, printing or duplication costs, etc., may be included.

> In the XYZ example, there are no significant miscellaneous costs.

f. The result is the **Consumable Materials Costs** per year.

Consumable Materials Costs Worksheet

XYZ Company _____

a. Number of Students/Class _____20_____ (a) _____

b. Consumable Materials
   Cost/Student   x   _____6_____ (b) _____

c. Number of Classes   x   _____12____ (c) _____

d. Consumable Materials
   Subtotal   =   ___1,440___ (d) _____

e. Misc. Consumable Materials + _____0_____ (e) _____

f. **Consumable Materials Costs** = ___1,440___ (f) _____

Revision/Update Costs

Revision/Update costs, although not an initial training cost consideration, must not be omitted when calculating costs for a non-development year.

This cost of on-going course maintenance has been looked upon as almost non-existent—and, that is the case for courses that undergo few changes over months or years. However, the Information Age is changing the assumption that a training course should enjoy a long life.

Procedure

a. Enter the **Total Instructional Development Costs/Year**. (May be found on Line **h** of the Instructional Development Costs Worksheet.)

b. Multiply by the **Revision Factor** for the current year.

    In our example, XYZ expects to have a 10% revision factor each year of its course life. We multiply by 0.10.

c. The result is the **Total Revision/Update Costs**.

Revision Costs Worksheet

XYZ Company _____

a. Total Instructional
   Development Costs/Year   _____143,103_____ (a) _____

b. Revision Factor (current year) x   _____.10_____ (b) _____

c. **Total Revision Costs**   =   _____14,310_____ (c) _____

Total Maintenance Costs

To obtain the total maintenance cost, add the bottom lines from each of the maintenance cost areas below:

a. Administrative Costs

b. Consumable Materials Costs

c. Revision Costs

d. Then add any Miscellaneous Maintenance Costs, including any contracted maintenance on training equipment.
   There were no miscellaneous maintenance costs for XYZ Company.

e. The result is Total Maintenance Costs.

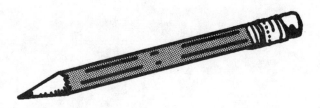

Maintenance Costs Worksheet

		XYZ Company	
a. Total Administrative Costs	+	3,406	(a)
b. Total Consumable Materials Costs	+	1,440	(b)
c. Total Revision Costs	+	14,310	(c)
d. Misc. Maintenance Costs	+	0	(d)
e. Total Maintenance Costs	=	19,156	(e)

NOTES

10. Formulating the Recommendation

NOTES

Recall that the objective of using the Training Cost Model is to enable you to:

- identify the costs of existing training programs,
- project the costs of proposed training programs, and
- compare the costs of using different methods for the same training.

In working with the XYZ Company example, we have accomplished the first objective: we have identified the costs of an existing training program.

As you may remember, the XYZ cost analysis was prompted by a staff member's suggestion to convert the existing instructor-led training course to a computer-based training (CBT) version. Therefore, the next step (after assuring ourselves that CBT is an *effective* method) would be to project the costs of the proposed program. However, rather than going through the analysis again for the proposed course, we will use some "guesstimates" so that the focus will be on the third objective, the comparison of costs.

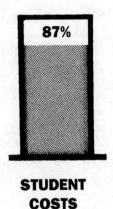

**STUDENT
COSTS**

On the Total Training Costs Worksheet, XYZ's overall expenses for the existing training program add up to $1,764,531. As you can see, an additional column has been added to this Worksheet to reflect the percentage of contribution to total training cost by each of the expense categories.

Notice that Student Costs equal 87 percent of the total cost of training. Clearly, here is a prime area to realize significant savings. The most direct way to reduce student costs is to shorten training time.

Total Training Costs Worksheet

	XYZ Company	%		%
Student Costs	1,526,400	87		
Instructor Costs	+ 55,872	3		
Instructional Development Costs (Amortized)	+ 143,103	8		
Facilities Costs	+ 20,000	1		
Maintenance Costs	+ 19,156	1		
Total Training Costs	= 1,764,531	100		
Annual Number of Students	÷ 240			
Annual Cost Per Student	= 7,352			

Student Costs

Individualized, performance-based instruction (such as CBT) can reduce course length by 30-60 percent of conventional instructor-led class time, according to many recent studies. In the XYZ example, the proposed training course was planned for four days—a 50 percent reduction in the existing course length. To estimate roughly the new student cost, we multiply Student Costs by .5 and enter the result ($763,200) on the Student Costs line on the XYZ Training Cost Comparison Worksheet, in the column marked CBT Version.

Instructor Costs

Obviously, when training time is reduced for students, it is reduced as well for instructors. When the method is changed from instructor-led to self-paced training, instructors may or may not be required to facilitate the learning process. In the case of XYZ Company, instructors would still be assigned to monitor a centralized self-study area or learning center. Because XYZ's proposed course would be reduced in time by 50 percent, we multiply Instructor Costs by .5 and enter $27,936 in the CBT Version column.

Training Costs Comparison Worksheet

	Existing Crs.	%	CBT Version	%
Student Costs	1,526,400	87	763,200	
Instructor Costs +	55,872	3	27,936	
Instructional Development Costs (Amortized) +				
Facilities Costs +				
Maintenance Costs +				
Total Training Costs =				
Annual Number of Students ÷				
Annual Cost Per Student =				

Instructional Development Costs

The resources needed for developing individualized instruction—and especially computer-based training—are generally far greater than those required for developing instructor-led courses.

In the case of XYZ Company, you may remember from the example, development costs were estimated at $550,000. This included equipment as well as contracting for the development to be completed in six months. When development costs are amortized over the remaining 2.5 years of the life of the course ($550,000 ÷ 2.5), the annual cost comes to $220,000—a substantial increase over the existing course's development costs.

Facilities Costs

A savings in facilities costs would be expected if course changes permitted the original facility to be available for other courses or other uses. In the case of XYZ's proposed course, the original facility would continue to be used as a learning center. Because of the specialized equipment involved, the facility would remain dedicated to this course. Therefore, the facilities costs would remain the same.

At a later date, however, the specialized hands-on equipment could be partitioned off from the CBT terminals to create a multi-purpose learning center. Thus, the cost of both the facility and the computer hardware (instructional development cost) could be spread over a number of uses, reducing the cost of this particular course.

Training Costs Comparison Worksheet

	Existing Crs.	%	CBT Version	%
Student Costs	1,526,400	87	763,200	___
Instructor Costs +	55,872	3	27,936	___
Instructional Development Costs (Amortized) +	143,103	8	220,000	___
Facilities Costs +	20,000	1	20,000	___
Maintenance Costs +	_____	__	_____	___
Total Training Costs =	_____	__	_____	___
Annual Number of Students ÷	_____		_____	
Annual Cost Per Student =	_____		_____	

Maintenance Costs

When an instructor-led course is converted to one that is computer-based, maintenance costs are almost always affected. Revision costs tend to be higher because of the extra effort required to program and debug changes in the computer course. Consumable materials costs are lower if the paper materials used in the instructor-led class are incorporated into the computer lessons. Administrative costs also are generally lower— especially in the clerical area, because of the built-in administrative functions of most CBT systems.

Expenses may increase substantially in the Miscellaneous Costs area, where an additional requirement for equipment maintenance and such substantial additional expenses as telecommunications charges must be taken into account.

For XYZ Company, an estimated $49,000 would be necessary to cover annual maintenance costs for the CBT course.

Projected Total Training Costs

When the costs in the five cost categories for the proposed CBT Version are totaled, an estimated annual expenditure is shown of $1,080,136—a reduction of $684,395 in the annual cost of the existing course. When analyzed on a per student basis, the annual cost declines from $7,352 for the existing course to $4,501 for the CBT version—a savings of $2,851 per student!

Training Costs Comparison Worksheet

		Existing Crs.	%	CBT Version	%
Student Costs		1,526,400	87	763,200	71
Instructor Costs	+	55,872	3	27,936	3
Instructional Development Costs (Amortized)	+	143,103	8	220,000	20
Facilities Costs	+	20,000	1	20,000	2
Maintenance Costs	+	19,156	1	49,000	5
Total Training Costs	=	1,764,531	100	1,080,136	101
Annual Number of Students	÷	240		240	
Annual Cost Per Student	=	7,352		4,501	

TRAINING COSTS COMPARISON WORKSHEET

The Recommendation

The purpose of training is to prepare an individual to perform effectively. We have a responsibility to provide training that works and enhances that individual's potential to be an excellent employee. No training recommendation should be made on the basis of short-term dollar savings alone. Other factors must be considered such as effectiveness, organizational climate, and your own personal goals. Only you are in a position to identify and evaluate those additional considerations.

Factors that may apply to any recommendation include:

* the potential of the proposed training to support other training needs:
    For XYZ Company, this may mean that a new computer-based system would provide administrative support for other ongoing courses, thus reducing the paperwork burden ordinarily placed on instructors. Or, the system could be used for testing in other courses to diagnose areas in which employees might need further training. Or, the system could be used to convert other courses that might benefit from a computer-assisted instructional approach.

INCREASE EFFECTIVENESS AND EFFICIENCY

- the impact on the training staff:

    For XYZ, a change from instructor-led to computer-based training will have a major impact. Training developers will require extensive training themselves to update and maintain the contracted CBT course. Instructors will require training to sharpen counseling and coaching skills needed to meet the needs of the individual learner, rather than those needed to address the requirements of group-paced classes. Instructors may look upon this as threatening or they may perceive it as a professional growth opportunity. You may influence that attitude.

- the potential for increased productivity or service levels:

    For XYZ Company, this potential exists in three areas: shorter time in the classroom could mean more time on the job responding to customer needs; reduced overtime might improve employee satisfaction; more precise testing made possible by the use of the computer could provide important diagnoses of employees' strengths and areas that need improvement. Perhaps XYZ will be able to stop the cancellation of orders, a $20 million loss last year.

You may want to present your argument for a CBT system based upon its potential impact on earnings per share and corporate profit. Let's assume that the XYZ company had $175 million in total income last year according to the annual report. The total cost for company operations and sales was $160 million for a profit of $15 million. One way to present the impact of CBT is to show graphically income projections with and without CBT. The company accounting department will be able to help you do this and their coordinated input will be valuable in your arguments.

If the projections are shown for 4 years, (the projected life of this course) the impact of CBT may be easily displayed. For example:

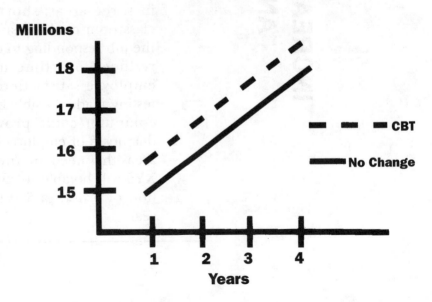

Additionally, it may be valuable to indicate the impact upon earnings per share. You may do this simply by dividing the annual profit by the number of shares outstanding. Assume the XYZ company has 30,000,000 shares outstanding. The earnings without CBT were $.50 each. With CBT the earnings would have been $.52, an increase of 4%. Using the profit projections from the above graph, the difference in earnings per share might be depicted as follows:

4 YEAR EARNINGS PER SHARE PROJECTION

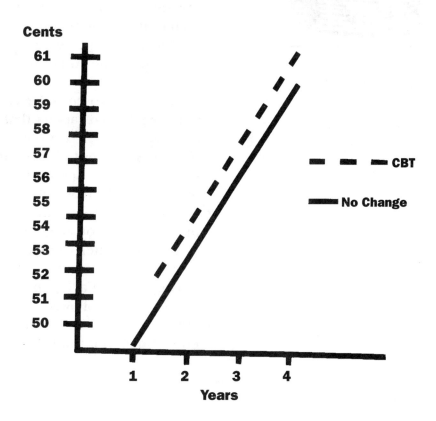

An increase of two cents per share in earnings for a company of this size *as a result of a single training course* is very significant. You also might point out that the cumulative impact over four years is $2,737,580 in increased profit!

The bottom line of the recommendation for XYZ Company:

Get started on the CBT Version!!

If you have been working on your own comparison, be sure to carefully repeat all of the steps in each of the five cost areas for each of the versions you are comparing. Then use the Training Cost Comparison Worksheet provided in the Appendix to conclude your analysis.

Remember to **consider carefully** all of the non-cost related factors that are unique and important to your own organization. Numbers may not always support your decisions. They are useful for evaluating the cost increase or decrease of alternatives you may be considering, but are never the complete picture. Also, you may want to recheck your assumptions after you have some real data to replace numbers you may have only estimated during your initial comparison.

If you have followed all of the steps in this guide, you may feel confident that your recommendation is founded on sound analysis.

Appendix

These worksheets are part of the
Training Cost Analysis model presented
in this book. You are encouraged to
modify them to meet your specific needs.

NOTES

Data Worksheets

Date _____

Course _____

Cost factor _____

Contact_____

Phone _____

Final data to be entered on worksheet_____

_____

Data Worksheets

Date _____

Course _____

Cost factor _____

Contact_____

Phone _____

Final data to be entered on worksheet_____

NOTES

Basic Cost Factors

- Course medium:
- Expected course life:
- Course length:
- Number in each class:
- Times course held each year:
- Geographic location of course:
- Facilities costs:
- Average annual salary:
  Students
  Instructors
  Instructional designers
  Subject matter experts
  Clerical staff
  Project leader
  Manager
- Annual productive days:
- Company's fringe benefits %:
- Average per diem expenses:
  Students
  Instructors
- Average travel expenses:
  Students
  Instructors
- Number of instructors per class:
- Development time:
  Project leader
  Instructional designer
  Subject matter expert
  Manager
  Clerical
- Administrative time:
  Manager
  Clerical
- Production costs:
- Materials costs:
  One-time
  Consumable
- Evaluation costs:
- Revision %:

NOTES

Student Costs Worksheet

a. Student Annual Salary	_____ (a)	_____
b. Fringe Benefits Factor	x _____ (b)	_____
c. Annual Productive Days	÷ _____ (c)	_____
d. Student Daily Salary	= _____ (d)	_____
e. Student Per Diem	+ _____ (e)	_____
f. Class Length (days)	x _____ (f)	_____
g. Salary Per Student Per Class	= _____ (g)	_____
h. Student Travel Costs	+ _____ (h)	_____
i. Lost Opportunity Cost	+ _____ (i)	_____
j. Total Number of Students	x _____ (j)	_____
k. Student Costs Subtotal	= _____ (k)	_____
l. Miscellaneous Student Costs	+ _____ (l)	_____
m. **Total Student Costs (Annual)**	= _____ (m)	_____

NOTES

Instructor Costs Worksheet

a. Instructor Annual Salary   _____ (a) _____

b. Fringe Benefits Factor   x _____ (b) _____

c. Annual Productive Days   ÷ _____ (c) _____

d. Instructor Daily Salary   = _____ (d) _____

e. Instructor Per Diem   + _____ (e) _____

f. Class Length (days)   x _____ (f) _____

g. Salary Per Instructor Per Class = _____ (g) _____

h. Number of Classes   x _____ (h) _____

i. Instructor Travel Costs   + _____ (i) _____

j. Lost Opportunity Cost   + _____ (j) _____

k. Total Number of Instructors   x _____ (k) _____

l. Instructor Costs Subtotal   = _____ (l) _____

m. Miscellaneous Instructor Costs + _____ (m) _____

n. Total Instructor Costs (Annual) = _____ (n) _____

NOTES

Instructional Development
Personnel Costs Worksheet

a. Project Leader Annual Salary   _____ (a) _____
b. Fringe Benefits Factor   x _____ (b) _____
c. Annual Productive Days   ÷ _____ (c) _____
d. Project Leader Daily Salary   = _____ (d) _____
e. Number of Days on Project   x _____ (e) _____
f. Project Leader Costs   = _____ **(f)** _____

g. Inst. Designer Annual Salary   _____ (g) _____
h. Fringe Benefits Factor   x _____ (h) _____
i. Annual Productive Days   ÷ _____ (i) _____
j. Inst. Designer Daily Salary   = _____ (j) _____
k. Number of Days on Project   x _____ (k) _____
l. Instructional Designer Costs = _____ **(l)** _____

m. Subj. Matter Exp. Annual Salary _____ (m) _____
n. Fringe Benefits Factor   x _____ (n) _____
o. Annual Productive Days   ÷ _____ (o) _____
p. SME Daily Salary   = _____ (p) _____
q. Number of Days on Project   x _____ (q) _____
r. Subject Matter Expert Costs = _____ **(r)** _____

s. Manager Annual Salary   _____ (s) _____
t. Fringe Benefits Factor   x _____ (t) _____
u. Annual Productive Days   ÷ _____ (u) _____
v. Manager Daily Salary   = _____ (v) _____
w. Number of Days on Project   x _____ (w) _____
x. Manager Costs   = _____ **(x)** _____

y. Clerical Annual Salary   _____ (y) _____
z. Fringe Benefits Factor   x _____ (z) _____
aa. Annual Productive Days   ÷ _____ (aa) _____
bb. Clerical Daily Salary   = _____ (bb) _____
cc. Number of Days on Project   x _____ (cc) _____
dd. Clerical Costs   = _____ **(dd)** _____
ee. Total Instructional Develop-
**   ment Personnel Costs**   = _____ **(ee)** _____

NOTES

Instructional Development Costs Worksheet

a. Personnel Costs   _____ (a)_____

b. Production and Materials Costs + _____ (b)_____

c. Evaluation Costs   + _____ (c)_____

d. Instructional Development
   Subtotal   = _____ (d)_____

e. Misc. Instructional Development
   Costs   + _____ (e)_____

f. Instructional Development Costs = _____ (f) _____

g. Amortization   ÷ _____ (g)_____

**h. Total Instructional Development
Costs Per Year**   = _____ **(h)**_____

NOTES

Facilities Costs Worksheet

	_____ _____
a. Annual Facilities Costs	_____ (a) _____
b. Course Allocation	x _____ (b) _____
c. Total Facilities Costs	= _____ (c) _____

NOTES

Administrative Costs Worksheet

a. Manager Annual Salary   _____   (a) _____

b. Fringe Benefits Factor   x   _____   (b) _____

c. Percent of Manager's Time   x   _____   (c) _____

d. Manager Costs Per Year   =   _____   (d) _____

e. Clerical Annual Salary   _____   (e) _____

f. Fringe Benefits Factor   x   _____   (f) _____

g. Percent of Clerical Time   x   _____   (g) _____

h. Clerical Costs Per Year   =   _____   (h) _____

i. Manager Costs Per Year   +   _____   **(i)** _____

j. Total Administrative Costs   =   _____   **(j)** _____

NOTES

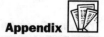

Consumable Materials Costs Worksheet

a. Number of Students/Class		_____	(a) _____
b. Consumable Materials Cost/Student	x	_____	(b) _____
c. Number of Classes	x	_____	(c) _____
d. Consumable Materials Subtotal	=	_____	(d) _____
e. Misc. Consumable Materials	+	_____	(e) _____
f. Consumable Materials Costs	=	_____	**(f)** _____

NOTES

Revision Costs Worksheet

a. Total Instructional
   Development Costs/Year   _____ (a) _____

b. Revision Factor (current year) x   _____ (b) _____

c. Total Revision Costs   =   _____ (c) _____

NOTES

Maintenance Costs Worksheet

_____   _____

a. Total Administrative Costs   +   _____   (a) _____

b. Total Consumable Materials
    Costs   +   _____   (b) _____

c. Total Revision Costs   +   _____   (c) _____

d. Misc. Maintenance Costs   +   _____   (d) _____

e. Total Maintenance Costs   =   _____   **(e)** _____

NOTES

Total Training Costs Worksheet

                                                      _____ %

Student Costs   _____ __

Instructor Costs   +   _____ __

Instructional Development
Costs (Amortized)   +   _____ __

Facilities Costs   +   _____ __

Maintenance Costs   +   _____ __

Total Training Costs   =   _____ __

Annual Number of Students ÷   _____

Annual Cost Per Student   =   _____

NOTES

Training Costs Comparison Worksheet

		_____ %	_____ %
Student Costs		_____ __	_____ __
Instructor Costs	+	_____ __	_____ __
Instructional Development Costs (Amortized)	+	_____ __	_____ __
Facilities Costs	+	_____ __	_____ __
Maintenance Costs	+	_____ __	_____ __
Total Training Costs	=	_____ __	_____ __
Annual Number of Students	÷	_____	_____
Annual Cost Per Student	=	_____	_____

NOTES

About the Author

Glenn E. Head holds degrees from Texas A&M University in Business Management and Educational Psychology. He served in the United States Air Force from 1973 through 1979. The USAF Chief of Staff and the Secretary of the Air Force honored him as the Outstanding Management Engineering Officer in the Air Force in 1975. Four years later, he was awarded the Meritorious Service Medal for outstanding contributions in the field of instructional technology.

In 1979 Glenn left the Air Force and founded Instructional Communications, Incorporated (ICOM) to provide high quality instructional products. ICOM has provided extensive services—including training cost analysis—to a large number of clients from its offices in Denver and Baltimore.

In 1990 Glenn co-founded New World Design Center as a place to conduct his expanded work in Social Architecture. He works with a few organizations each year that choose to go beyond business as usual, to begin the process of uncovering the full potential of their people and the organization. His passion is in assisting leaders to uncover and express a vision and purpose that will carry their organization forward for over 100 years.

Glenn has been and is an active leader in a number of professional organizations, including the American Society for Training and Development (ASTD), the National Society for Performance and Instruction (NSPI) and the Association for Development of Computer-based Instructional Systems (ADCIS), where he served seven years as a National Officer and was President in 1988-89.

NOTES

NOTES

NOTES

NOTES

NOTES